The Son Who Swallowed the Moon

By

C. Raymond

Copyright © 2025 by – C. Raymond - All Rights Reserved.

It is not legal to reproduce, duplicate, or transmit any part of this document in either electronic means or printed format. Recording of this publication is strictly prohibited.

Dedication

This book is dedicated to the silent warriors: the ones who carry unseen burdens, who smile through hidden pain, and who strive daily to break the invisible chains of generational curses. To my ancestors, whose voices echo within me, guiding my steps toward freedom and self-discovery. To my mother, grandmother, sisters, and my father for your resilience and strength and for teaching me the meaning of sacrifice and survival. And to every Black gay man navigating spaces where your worth and authenticity are constantly challenged—this book is your beacon; let it remind you that you are seen, valued, and profoundly powerful.

Acknowledgment

I first acknowledge God's grace for giving me the strength to confront my shadows and for illuminating my path with clarity and purpose.

To my grandmother, whose stories sparked a deeper understanding of my lineage and whose wisdom anchors me. Your quiet strength has shown me the beauty in vulnerability and truth.

To my mother, who taught me to navigate life's complexities even through her own struggles. Your resilience has shaped my heart and spirit.

To my sisters, my dad, and every figure who stepped into roles when others stepped out—you've shown me the many faces of courage.

I am deeply grateful to those who stood beside me during my darkest hours, those who offered me mirrors rather than judgments, and who taught me the power of love and vulnerability. To everyone who supported me through this process, your presence and encouragement have been invaluable.

A special acknowledgment to the teachings that found me—esoteric wisdom, astrology, Tarot, and the philosophies of interconnectedness. These studies became the bridge to understanding myself and my shadows profoundly.

Lastly, to every reader embarking on their own journey of healing: thank you for your bravery. Your willingness to dive into your shadows and rise into your truth is the greatest inspiration behind this work.

About the Author

C. Raymond is a deeply introspective writer, music artist, and passionate advocate for transformative healing through shadow work. Born and raised in the vibrant yet challenging atmosphere of Washington, D.C., Raymond's personal experiences with familial struggles, identity exploration, and the pursuit of spiritual clarity profoundly shaped his worldview.

Raymond's early life was marked by navigating complex emotional landscapes—growing up amidst the echoes of generational trauma, absent father figures, and societal pressures. His journey as a Black man in communities often hesitant to embrace full authenticity provided him with unique insights into the power of self-acceptance, resilience, and unconditional self-compassion.

His creative endeavors extend beyond writing into music production, reflecting his belief in the transformative power of artistic expression. Drawing heavily on esoteric teachings, astrology, and Tarot, Raymond uses his multifaceted experiences to help others uncover their own hidden truths. His work aims to dismantle barriers of shame and silence, guiding others toward self-empowerment, community healing, and a renewed sense of purpose.

With authenticity and vulnerability at the core of his message, Raymond continues to inspire others to confront their shadows bravely and to embrace every aspect of their humanity in their quest for deeper meaning and profound healing.

Table Of Contents

Part I: The Descent—Unveiling the Shadow

1. **Roots of the Shadow** – Understanding the foundation of abandonment, father wounds, and identity loss

2. **The Fractured Self: The Intersection of Masculinity and Emotional Repression** – The silent expectations that shape men and suppress emotions

3. **Reflections of the Father** – The psychological impact of father wounds and the struggle to break toxic cycles

Part II: Confrontation—Walking Through the Abyss

4. **The Abyss and the Ascent** – Facing self-sabotage, toxic relationship patterns, and the moments that force transformation

5. **Ancestral Wisdom and Karma** – The inherited pain we carry and the responsibility to break generational cycles.

6. **The Universal Mind and Collective Consciousness** – The interconnected nature of trauma, healing, and the unseen forces that guide us.

Part III: Integration—Reclaiming the Hidden Self

7. **The Cycles of Existence: Birth, Death, and Rebirth** – Dying to old identities and stepping into transformation.

8. **Building Empathy and Compassion** – Learning to extend grace to ourselves and others as we heal.

9. **The Hidden Knowledge Within Us** – Unlocking subconscious programming, esoteric wisdom, and the truth buried beneath conditioning.

Part IV: Embodiment—The Rebirth of the Self

10. **The Divine Current Within** – Understanding the sacred, energetic power within Blackness and spiritual identity.

11. **Reclaiming the Sacred Feminine & Masculine Balance** – Integrating both energies for true personal and relational healing.

12. **Transforming Pain into Power** – Alchemizing wounds into wisdom and breaking

free from destructive cycles

Part V: The Journey Continues

13. **The Ongoing Journey** – Shadow work as a lifelong commitment and the invitation to continue evolving

Part VI: Epilogue – A Whisper Beyond the Page

PREFACE

I did not set out to write this book. Shadow work found me the same way darkness follows the setting sun—inevitable, all-consuming, patient in its arrival. It was never a matter of if I would face my shadow, but when. Like many, I spent years avoiding my reflection, numbing wounds that refused to be ignored, mistaking survival for healing. But shadows do not disappear in avoidance. They wait.

This book is not just a collection of thoughts—it is an excavation, a reclamation of every part of me I once abandoned. It is a journey through generational cycles, through wounds inherited and wounds self-inflicted, through the quiet moments where truth reveals itself, unfiltered and raw. It is about becoming whole, not perfect. About embracing the parts of ourselves that society, culture, and even our own families have taught us to suppress.

Shadow work is not comfortable. It is not gentle. It does not promise a neatly wrapped resolution. But it is honest. And in honesty, there is liberation.

This book is an offering to those who have felt lost in their own reflections, who have questioned their worth, who have walked through fire and wondered if there was anything left on the other side. I have walked that path. I am still walking it. And if you are here, then perhaps you are, too.

May these words be a mirror. May they be a map. And above all, may they remind you that even in the deepest shadows, there is always light waiting to be found.

Chapter 1: Roots of the Shadow

I was born into a world of ghosts—men who were present in name but missing in spirit. My father was one of them. His absence shaped me before I even had the words to name it. Raised in a single-parent household with my mother, sisters, and grandmother, I learned early that survival meant adaptation. Masculinity, self-worth, and love were not things I was taught; they were riddles I had to solve in the quiet moments between responsibilities. My father sent money but rarely his presence. I remember waiting on porches, watching headlights drift past, my heart pounding at the thought that maybe this time he would come. But the streetlights flickered on, and I knew the answer. He wasn't coming.

Abandonment was the first lesson I learned, long before love.

The Weight of My Childhood

I can still remember sitting in trap houses while my father sold drugs, watching him move in and out of different lives while never fully being present in mine. I was just a child, absorbing everything—his charm, his recklessness, his detachment. He had money, he had women, but he never had time. He would send his friends to check in on me, buy me things when he couldn't be there himself. And at first, that made me feel special—like I was being looked after by men who had some loyalty to my father, to me. But one by one, they disappeared. Just like him, they became ghosts, failing to show up when I needed them the most.

When both my parents were absent, my grandmother took us in. I became the eldest man in the house, even though I was still just a child. I got my sisters ready for school, braided their hair, ironed their clothes, and made sure they ate. Inside, I felt the weight of responsibility crushing me, but outside, I was still a boy running the streets, playing sports, fighting when I had to. I had to be tough; there was no room to be weak. My mother was a tomboy, running the streets with my uncles, hustling, drinking, and surviving in her own way. When she was home, she was always moving, always looking for the next opportunity, the next way to keep us afloat. She did her best, but she was just like my father in a different form. They were both chasing something and in their chase, I got left behind.

One Christmas, everything changed. We were used to extravagant holidays, so many gifts piled up that you could barely walk through the living room. But that year, my mother was struggling. The presents were few, and I could see the disappointment in my sisters' faces. My mother, who always held it together, broke down crying in front of us. That was the moment I stopped caring about holidays. That was the moment I understood what struggle felt like, the shame of not having enough. The weight of that day never left me.

And then there was the day I told my mother I was gay. She locked herself in her room for three days.

She didn't want to believe it because she had seen me with women. She wanted something else for me. And even though she told me she still loved me, I could see the disappointment in her eyes. I could feel the distance between us grow. In the Black community, masculinity is already fragile, and to be a Black gay man is to live in a space where people question your worth, your strength, your very place in the world. My father, already distant, became even more so, ashamed in a way he never voiced, but I could feel it in his silence.

The Shadow and Its Teachings

In esoteric thought, the shadow is not something to be feared—it is a guide, a teacher. It holds the unprocessed pain, the generational wounds, and the wisdom waiting to be reclaimed. The shadow is the aspect of self that society, culture, and family have forced into silence. It exists as the subconscious manifestation of all the parts of me that were rejected: the boy who wanted love, the man who sought belonging, the spirit that longed to be whole.

Sitting in those trap houses, I was unknowingly absorbing the power of illusion—the same illusion found in ancient teachings of duality, where light and darkness must coexist. My father was a master of illusion, appearing and disappearing at will, his presence felt more in absence than in reality. He was both shadow and substance, much like the celestial bodies that guide the cycles of the universe—the moon, waxing and waning, always present yet never fully seen.

The abandonment I felt was not just my own, but a story written long before I was born. The sins of the father become the burdens of the son unless they are transmuted. This is the alchemy of shadow work—the ability to take inherited pain and turn it into wisdom, to break cycles rather than be broken by them. I had to see the absence not as a void but as an invitation to reclaim myself. My father's distance forced me to seek my own light, just as the moon must reflect the sun to be seen.

The Depth of the Shadow

I learned that the parts of myself I ignored didn't disappear; they only grew stronger in the background, shaping my thoughts, my reactions, and my relationships. Every rejection, every moment of feeling unseen, every abandonment—those memories didn't fade; they lived inside me, pushing me to protect myself at all costs. I built walls so high that even I struggled to climb over them.

But the truth is, the shadow isn't something to be feared. It isn't some separate part of me that needs to be erased. It is the sum of my experiences, the parts of me that weren't accepted, the wounds that never healed. It is the part of me that learned to survive, to keep moving, to keep pushing forward even when everything inside me screamed to stop. And yet, that same shadow also holds my power. The pain I've endured has given me wisdom. The darkness I've walked through has sharpened my vision.

Shadow work isn't just about self-exploration—it's about breaking cycles. It's about understanding that trauma is inherited, just as resilience is. The pain endured by my ancestors did not start with me, but it continues through me unless I choose to end it. There is healing in reclaiming the lost parts of ourselves, in facing what we fear, and in giving voice to the silence that was forced upon us.

For years, I carried the wounds of my father's absence like an heirloom, passing them down to my relationships, my self-worth, and my perception of love. But shadow work is the great alchemy—the process of transmuting pain into power. It is the decision to look into the mirror, to see what has been hidden, and to reclaim the pieces of ourselves we were taught to reject.

Like the hidden texts of ancient wisdom traditions, the answers are buried, waiting for those willing to seek them. My shadow was not just mine—it was an accumulation of generational wounds, of cultural silencing, of spiritual lessons waiting to be unearthed. There came a moment when I could no longer carry the weight of resentment. I had to choose healing. I had to redefine what love, worth, and masculinity meant to me—not by what was missing, but by what I could create.

Reflective Journal Prompts

1. What childhood experiences have shaped my fears, doubts, or beliefs about myself?

2. How have generational traumas influenced my current mindset and relationships?

3. In what ways have I internalized the shadows of my ancestors?

4. What esoteric or spiritual practices can help me reclaim my lost power?

5. How can I transmute my pain into strength, wisdom, and purpose?

Chapter 1
Roots of The Shadows

Affirmation: The pain I inherited is not my prison; it is the soil from which I rise.

1. What childhood experiences have shaped my fears, doubts, or beliefs about myself?

_____
_____
_____
_____
_____
_____
_____
_____
_____

2. How have generational traumas influenced my current mindset and relationships?

_____
_____
_____
_____
_____
_____
_____
_____
_____

Affirmation: The pain I inherited is not my prison; it is the soil from which I rise.

3. In what ways have I internalized the shadows of my ancestors?

_____
_____
_____
_____
_____
_____
_____
_____
_____

4. What esoteric or spiritual practices can help me reclaim my lost power?

_____
_____
_____
_____
_____
_____
_____
_____
_____
_____

Affirmation: The pain I inherited is not my prison; it is the soil from which I rise.

5. How can I transmute my pain into strength, wisdom, and purpose?

Chapter 2: The Fractured Self—The Intersection of Masculinity and Emotional Repression

The Silent Rules of Manhood

I was never explicitly told to suppress my emotions. No one sat me down and said, "Don't cry" or "Don't show how you feel." But I never needed to be told. The lesson was already there, unspoken but absolute: **men don't cry.**

I saw it in the way the men in my family carried themselves. Even in moments of grief, even at funerals, tears were a private thing—if they came at all. Strength was measured in silence, in the ability to keep moving forward no matter how much something hurt. If pain existed, it was locked away. If fear crept in, it was buried beneath a hard exterior. And if love was ever present, it was something you proved through action, not through words.

My father was a boxer, and like him, I was put into the ring. I learned to channel every emotion into my fists, to hit harder, to move faster, to keep my guard up—literally and figuratively. In the gym, there was no room for softness. There was power, there was endurance, there was skill—but vulnerability? That was a liability. I fought not just for sport but as an outlet for everything I was never allowed to express.

But outside of the ring, that armor didn't come off. Even at home, I had to be strong. I grew up around women, and being the only boy in the house meant I had a role to play. I had to be the protector, the one who didn't break, the one who held things together. There was no space for weakness, no room to question who I was. I just had to **be hard.**

It's said in esoteric traditions that the energy we suppress does not vanish—it transforms and finds other ways to manifest. Ancient mystics spoke of **the duality within us all**—the masculine and feminine, the solar and the lunar, the active and the receptive. But I had been conditioned to reject one side of myself, believing that to embrace emotion was to lose power. In truth, the refusal to feel was what weakened me. The shadow self does not disappear just because you ignore it; it waits. And when it returns, it demands to be acknowledged.

The Cost of Emotional Suppression

For most of my teenage years, I didn't have an outlet. I didn't have anyone to confide in, and there was no safe space to process the things I was feeling. When I left home and moved to North Carolina to live with my great aunt and uncle, I was suddenly in a slower environment, away from everything I knew in D.C. That isolation made me suppress my emotions even more. Without family around to lean on, I found brotherhood in the hood, in the streets, in places where I had to be extra masculine to survive.

I followed the blueprint laid out by my parents—selling drugs, partying, running from any real confrontation with myself. But the truth was, no matter how much I tried to play the role, I was still hiding.

I sought validation in relationships. I was with older men who could provide for me and women who fit the image of who I was supposed to be. I was looking for something I didn't even fully understand—maybe a father figure, maybe acceptance, maybe just a way to quiet the voice in my head telling me I was living a lie.

In esoteric teachings, our **external reality is a projection of our internal state**. When we live in suppression, the world reflects that suppression back to us. My environment—filled with hyper-masculine energy, secrecy, and survival—was not separate from my inner world. It was a manifestation of it. The Kabbalistic concept of the **Tree of Life** speaks of balance, of the need for both structure and mercy, force and surrender. But I had been living solely in force, trapped in the rigid framework of what a man was supposed to be, unable to see that true power comes not from resistance but from integration.

At night, though, the thoughts would creep in. I remember my first experience with a man, my mom's best friend's brother. We had the same birthday. In the moment, it felt exciting, but afterward, I was fighting demons, praying for God to take these feelings away from me. I wanted to be normal. I wanted to be what I had been taught a man was supposed to be.

I saw what happened to people who didn't fit the mold. I remember watching my dad fight a transgender woman in a trap house. I don't know what led to it, but I remember the way she hit him on the head with a glass bottle. That image stuck with me. It confirmed everything I had feared—being different came at a cost.

In esoteric traditions, there's an understanding that the **universe does not punish or reward—it reflects**. The pain we internalize becomes the pain we see in the world. My fear of being different, of being exposed, created a world where difference was dangerous. My shame became externalized in the people I saw suffer for simply existing. But in truth, the real suffering was the war within me.

Breaking the Cycle

The turning point came when I moved to Houston. I had left everything behind, and along with me came a man I was dating. I was thinking it would be a fresh start. But that relationship ended badly. He thought I was cheating, even though it was the only relationship where I had been faithful. It was like karma catching up to me—everything I had done in the past was now being done to me.

Suddenly, I was alone in Texas, with no real friends, no family, no backup plan. That's when I was forced to open up to my mom. I told her everything—about my sexuality and the things I had been carrying in silence for years. And for the first time, I felt close to her. I saw a softness in her I had never seen before. I felt **understood.**

There's a concept in mysticism that true healing comes when we embrace the full spectrum of who we are. The **shadow self must be acknowledged, not destroyed**. That moment with my mom was an initiation of sorts—an alchemical transformation where the old wounds began to turn into wisdom. The lead of my past, my repression, was finally being turned into gold.

Healing & Moving Forward

Integrating my emotions hasn't been easy. There are still moments when I shut down, when I overthink, when I catch myself slipping into old habits. But I've learned to catch myself. I've learned to self-reflect, to take accountability, to express myself before anger is the only thing left.

The biggest change has been in my relationships. My family dynamic may not have shifted much, but I've built a solid foundation of friends who truly understand me. I've found a space where I don't have to hide, where I don't have to prove anything, where I can just be **me.**

In the ancient teachings, there's an understanding that **we are both the seeker and the sought, the question and the answer.** I spent years searching for something outside of myself—love, validation, acceptance. But the truth is, everything I was looking for was already within me. I just had to be willing to look.

If I could talk to my younger self, I'd tell him this:

"You don't have to choose between masculinity and vulnerability. You don't have to fit into anyone's mold but your own. You are whole, just as you are."

And for the first time in my life, I believe it.

Healing is not a destination; it's a process, a continuous unraveling of the layers we've built around ourselves. There are still moments when I catch myself shutting down, slipping into old patterns of avoidance or emotional detachment. The difference now is that I notice it—I see my shadow, I recognize the walls before they grow too high. That awareness alone is power.

Shadow work has taught me that **true masculinity is not about dominance, nor is it about suppressing emotions—it's about integration.** Strength is not the absence of vulnerability but the courage to embrace it. I no longer see emotions as something to fear or something that weakens me. Instead, I see them as tools—guides that show me where healing still needs to happen.

I've learned that being a man is not about how much I can endure in silence but how willing I am to express, to evolve, to redefine my own sense of self. Masculinity, to me now, is **balance.** It is knowing when to be firm and when to be soft, when to lead and when to surrender, when to protect and when to allow myself to be protected.

I am still unlearning. I am still rebuilding. I am still peeling back layers, discovering new parts of myself, and facing emotions I once tried to escape. But for the first time in my life, I am not running. I am standing in my truth, unapologetically.

And for that, I am free.

Reflection Questions for Journaling

Early Conditioning & Masculinity:

1. What emotions have you been conditioned to suppress? How has that affected your relationships and sense of self?

2. Think of a specific moment in your childhood when you learned what it meant to "be a man." How did that moment shape you?

3. How did your male role models express (or not express) emotions? What messages did you receive from them about vulnerability?

Adolescence & Emotional Repression:

4. How did you cope with sadness, fear, or loneliness as a teenager? Have those coping mechanisms changed?

5. Was there ever a moment when you wanted to express your emotions but felt unable to? What stopped you?

6. What role did relationships—romantic or platonic—play in your emotional expression growing up?

Relationships & Communication:

7. How has emotional suppression impacted your romantic relationships? Have partners ever called you out on being emotionally unavailable?

8. What is the hardest emotion for you to express in relationships? Why?

9. How do you think your past wounds influence the type of people you attract into your life?

Breaking the Cycle:

10. What was the first time you allowed yourself to be vulnerable? How did it feel?

11. What beliefs about masculinity and emotions are you actively unlearning?

12. What new habits have you adopted to express emotions in a healthier way?

Healing & Moving Forward:

13. What does masculinity mean to you today? How has your definition evolved?

14. If you could speak to your younger self, what would you tell him about emotions, strength, and self-acceptance?

15. What are small but powerful ways you can practice emotional awareness and expression daily?

Final Thought:

This journey is yours alone, but you are not alone in it. The more you uncover, the more you heal, and the more you step into the fullness of who you are. Masculinity is not something to prove—it is something to embody, something to shape in your own image. You are both the seeker and the sought, the healer and the healed.

Your shadow is not your enemy. It is your guide.

Now, what will you do with what you've discovered?

Chapter 2
The Fractured Self—The Intersection of Masculinity and Emotional Repression

Affirmation: I give myself permission to feel—deeply, fully, and without shame.

1. What emotions have you been conditioned to suppress? How has that affected your relationships and sense of self?

_____
_____
_____
_____
_____
_____
_____
_____
_____

2. Think of a specific moment in your childhood when you learned what it meant to "be a man." How did that moment shape you?

_____
_____
_____
_____
_____
_____
_____
_____
_____
_____

Affirmation: I give myself permission to feel—deeply, fully, and without shame.

3. How did your male role models express (or not express) emotions? What messages did you receive from them about vulnerability?

....
....
....
....
....
....
....
....
....
....

4. How did you cope with sadness, fear, or loneliness as a teenager? Have those coping mechanisms changed?

....
....
....
....
....
....
....
....
....
....
....

Affirmation: I give myself permission to feel—deeply, fully, and without shame.

5. Was there ever a moment when you wanted to express your emotions but felt unable to? What stopped you?

....
....
....
....
....
....
....
....
....

6. What role did relationships—romantic or platonic—play in your emotional expression growing up?

....
....
....
....
....
....
....
....
....
....

Affirmation: I give myself permission to feel—deeply, fully, and without shame.

7. How has emotional suppression impacted your romantic relationships? Have partners ever called you out on being emotionally unavailable?

....
....
....
....
....
....
....
....
....
....
....

8. What is the hardest emotion for you to express in relationships? Why?

....
....
....
....
....
....
....
....
....
....
....

Affirmation: I give myself permission to feel—deeply, fully, and without shame.

9. How do you think your past wounds influence the type of people you attract into your life?

....
....
....
....
....
....
....
....
....
....

10. What was the first time you allowed yourself to be vulnerable? How did it feel?

....
....
....
....
....
....
....
....
....
....

Affirmation: I give myself permission to feel—deeply, fully, and without shame.

11. What beliefs about masculinity and emotions are you actively unlearning?

....
....
....
....
....
....
....
....
....
....

12. What new habits have you adopted to express emotions in a healthier way?

....
....
....
....
....
....
....
....
....
....

Affirmation: I give myself permission to feel—deeply, fully, and without shame.

13. What does masculinity mean to you today? How has your definition evolved?

_____
_____
_____
_____
_____
_____
_____
_____
_____

14. If you could speak to your younger self, what would you tell him about emotions, strength, and self-acceptance?

_____
_____
_____
_____
_____
_____
_____
_____
_____
_____

Affirmation: I give myself permission to feel—deeply, fully, and without shame.

15. What are small but powerful ways you can practice emotional awareness and expression daily?

....
....
....
....
....
....
....
....
....
....
....

Chapter 3: Reflections of the Father

The first thing I ever learned about love was that it could hurt. It could bruise and shatter; it could whisper promises and leave echoes of betrayal. I learned this not from my own experience but from the violent symphony of my parents' relationship. My father, a man who could command a room with his laughter and charm, was also a man who could empty it with his temper and his betrayals.

As far back as I can remember, my father had a history of cheating. My mother didn't fear him—she confronted him. She was a fighter in every sense of the word, never willing to cower, never one to let a man's choices define her. I remember the women he brought me around, thinking I was too young to understand, but I did. I was always too aware. His presence was fleeting, and when he was home, the air around him felt heavy, as if a storm was always threatening to break.

Though I don't recall witnessing the domestic violence between my parents firsthand, I knew it existed. I knew it from the way my mother's resilience hardened, from the way she carried herself, from the sharp edges of words left unspoken. I do remember, vividly, an altercation between my father and, my younger brother and sister's mother. That night, I peeked through a cracked door and saw her back slam against the floor as she tried to fight him off before the door violently shut. When you're young, you watch in fear; you know it's wrong. But when you see it enough, you become numb. It was in that numbness that I vowed never to be like my father.

That promise was tested when, as a teenager, my father came home from prison and stayed with us in Southeast D.C. A dispute erupted between my parents—its details blurred by time—and I, no longer just a silent observer, confronted him. His response was a punch to my chest. That moment shattered any illusion I had left of a father-son bond. I didn't know how to process my emotions then, and even now, I find myself having to sit with my feelings before I can express them. I choose my words carefully, not because I lack the ability to be bluntly honest, but because I have spent a lifetime trying to salvage the emotions of others, often at the expense of my own.

The Psychological Impact of Father Wounds

Despite my vow to be different, the echoes of my father's influence found their way into my own relationships. I have been in toxic and violent relationships where anger, betrayal, and miscommunication ignited flames that burned everything in their path. I have been nearly hit by a car, violently fought, shot at, and hit lovers with weapons in moments of rage. Though I never initiated the fights, my inability to communicate during moments of anger triggered my partners' reactions. My anger always seemed to take over, swallowing reason whole.

Generational trauma often repeats itself in patterns that feel inescapable. It is not just the behaviors we inherit but the emotional wounds that shape our relationships and self-perception. The fear of becoming my father turned into a subconscious cycle of resistance and reaction, never truly healing, only reinforcing what I wanted to escape. Breaking this cycle required stepping outside of survival mode and acknowledging the trauma without letting it define my future.

Shadow Work and Integration

Healing required more than recognition—it demanded integration. I had to learn that rejecting my father's influence entirely only gave it more power. True transformation came when I acknowledged the parts of myself shaped by him, not to accept them as my fate but to understand them as stepping stones toward my own growth. The work of facing my shadow meant embracing every emotion, every impulse, every moment of inherited anger, and choosing a different path.

I noticed how my patterns of anger and avoidance mirrored his. I wasn't striking out physically, but I fought with my words, with my silence, with my inability to allow myself to be vulnerable. My relationships bore the weight of my unhealed wounds. It wasn't just about controlling my temper; it was about learning to sit with my emotions without letting them consume me. I had to teach myself how to express frustration without aggression, how to trust without fear, and how to love without expecting betrayal.

Redefining Strength and Masculinity

For years, I wrestled with the concept of masculinity. I had been taught that dominance, control, and emotional detachment were signs of strength. I had seen what unchecked power looked like in a man, and I wanted no part of it. But rejecting masculinity altogether left me in conflict with myself. Healing meant redefining what it meant to be strong—not through force, but through emotional intelligence, patience, and resilience. Strength was not in the fists but in the ability to walk away. Power was not in control but in the capacity to be vulnerable without fear.

I thought back to the way my father carried himself—always commanding, always in control—but control that came from fear, from needing to assert dominance rather than earn respect. I had to learn that real strength wasn't about being feared but about being trusted. It wasn't about silencing others but about listening. I wanted to be the kind of man who could hold space for others, who could lead with compassion rather than intimidation.

The Turning Point: Choosing Peace Over Conflict

The moment that truly forced me to confront and begin healing from my father's influence was not a fight, but silence. When I got my own apartment, I invited my father over. I reached out several times.

He never answered. He never showed. That was when I became okay with his absence. That was when I realized I feared having children, not because I didn't want them, but because I never wanted to be like him.

Healing meant learning to walk away from conflict. It meant reclaiming my peace. It meant accepting that while my father was part of my story, he was not the author of my future. I have never had a conversation with him about his past actions because I know he would deny them. But I no longer need his validation or his apology.

The Role of Creativity in Healing

Through music, writing, and self-expression, I have reclaimed my narrative. I have learned that art has the power to turn pain into something meaningful, to transform trauma into wisdom. Every lyric I write, every story I tell, every moment I channel my past into something constructive—I take another step toward healing. The act of creation is my way of proving that I am more than my wounds, that I am the master of my own story.

A Vision for the Future

Healing is not about erasing the past but about learning from it. It is about taking the lessons that pain has offered and using them to build something better. I do not want to pass down cycles of trauma—I want to pass down resilience, love, and self-awareness. My journey is not about proving that I am different from my father; it is about proving to myself that I can be the kind of man I always needed.

When I look in the mirror now, I sometimes catch glimpses of my father in my mannerisms, in the way I carry myself. It makes me pause. When people tell me I look like him, my immediate response is always, 'I look better.' Because I do. Because I am better. Because I have chosen to be.

My closure is not in a letter, not in a conversation that will never happen, but in my actions. In my music. In my goals. In my commitment to improving myself mentally, spiritually, and physically. The reflection of the father is one that lingers, casting long shadows. But shadows only exist in the presence of light. And I am learning, day by day, that I am my own light.

Reflective Questions:

1. How has my father's influence shaped my perception of strength and masculinity?
2. What unconscious patterns have I repeated in my relationships, and how can I break them?

3. How can I transform past pain into a source of wisdom and power?

4. What does true healing look like for me, beyond just survival?

5. How can I redefine my legacy and choose a different path for the future?

Chapter 3
Reflections of the Father

Affirmation: I am safe to sit with my emotions—they are not my enemies.

1. How has my father's influence shaped my perception of strength and masculinity?

_____
_____
_____
_____
_____
_____
_____
_____
_____

2. What unconscious patterns have I repeated in my relationships, and how can I break them?

_____
_____
_____
_____
_____
_____
_____
_____
_____
_____

Affirmation: I am safe to sit with my emotions—they are not my enemies.

3. How can I transform past pain into a source of wisdom and power?

_____
_____
_____
_____
_____
_____
_____
_____
_____
_____

4. What does true healing look like for me, beyond just survival?

_____
_____
_____
_____
_____
_____
_____
_____
_____
_____

Affirmation: I am safe to sit with my emotions—they are not my enemies.

5. How can I redefine my legacy and choose a different path for the future?

Chapter 4: The Abyss and the Ascent

The deeper I went into my own darkness, the closer I came to discovering the light that had been buried underneath it all. But before I could rise, I had to surrender to the fall.

The Descent into the Abyss

There came a moment when everything I had buried inside could no longer be contained. The anger I silenced, the pain I numbed, the shame I masked with a smile—they rose like a tide I could no longer outrun. It wasn't a dramatic breakdown. It was quiet. Still. But inside, I was being torn open.

My shadow showed up most in the way I loved and the way I ran. In relationships, I struggled to communicate, leaned on sexual validation, and used money or gifts to fix what words could not. I was mirroring behaviors I once despised—especially those of my father. That realization shook me. I wasn't just repeating cycles. I was living inside them.

I'll never forget the woman I thought I would marry. We painted together, made shirts during the Jena 6 movement, explored art and activism like we were building a world of our own. It felt sacred, divinely timed. Our connection was more than chemistry—it felt like soul memory. Like we had done this dance before, in other lives, under other skies. She was my mirror and my muse. But when she found out I was gay, her silence said everything. I already struggled with feeling like I wasn't man enough, and now I had hurt someone I loved deeply. We stopped speaking. The guilt was overwhelming, knowing she got caught in my war with self-acceptance.

Now, through the lens of esoteric wisdom, I understand that our connection was far more than human love—it was a soul contract. She came into my life as a guide, as a mirror to reflect the illusion I had constructed. She didn't just hold my heart; she held a key to my spiritual awakening. Her love cracked the mask I wore and revealed the face I was terrified to see. Her silence became sacred. Her absence became alchemy.

This wasn't just heartbreak. It was initiation. The mystics speak of sacred rupture, of divine dismantling—the necessary destruction before rebirth. Her departure marked the beginning of that. It forced me to die to who I pretended to be so I could finally meet who I truly was.

Today, our connection is different. There's no need to reclaim what was because we both evolved. Her memory still stirs gratitude in me. I honor her not as a chapter I lost but as a portal I passed through. She was the threshold between my old self and the man I was becoming.

Patterns of Self-Sabotage

Insecurity bred self-sabotage. As a Black gay man, the pressure to look good, succeed professionally, and be emotionally strong felt suffocating. I remember freezing during a kindergarten talent show, unable to perform the MC Hammer dance I had practiced. I ran offstage and cried in the hallway. That feeling of not being enough followed me into adulthood.

I either gave too much or disappeared. I overcompensated by performing the version of me I thought others wanted. Or I ghosted, afraid they'd see the truth and walk away first. But through shadow work, I started reclaiming those lost fragments of myself. I took my fear of performance and turned it into power—on stage, in music, in life. What once paralyzed me now fuels me.

How My Shadow Shows Up in Relationships

Even now, when conflict arises, I still feel that urge to run. But I've learned to pause. To walk away in peace and come back in truth. Some may call it avoidance, but for me, it's regulation. I'm choosing not to let trauma speak for me.

Growing up, I was taught that vulnerability was weakness. That love was something you earned, not something you simply received. I never learned how to be emotionally safe, only how to survive. Shadow work has taught me to unlearn that. To speak up. To feel fully. To be seen without shame.

Breaking Generational Cycles

In my family, we didn't talk about wounds. We pushed through. We hid. I didn't even realize I had trauma until I started digging. My sister and I talk often about the cycles we're breaking—poverty, violence, emotional absence. She raises her kids with softness and presence, something we never had. That inspires me. We're rewriting our legacy with every honest conversation, every intentional act of care.

Breaking cycles isn't just about making money or achieving success. It's about choosing love over fear. Connection over avoidance. It's knowing that karma runs in bloodlines—but so does healing. And I've made it my mission to pass down something better.

Society and Shadow Suppression

The world doesn't make it easy to be whole. Social media praises surface-level performance, not inner work. Being a Black gay man means navigating expectations from every angle. Be strong. Be sexy. Be silent. I've chosen to reject all of that. I'd rather be honest than admired. I'd rather be whole than approved of.

I was taught not to cry. To be tough. To hold it all in. But that kind of masculinity is a cage. Shadow work cracked it open. Now, I give myself permission to feel. I allow space for softness. That's my revolution.

Healing and Integration

I used to think healing meant perfection. Now I know it means presence. It's recognizing when the shadow shows up and choosing to meet it with compassion instead of fear. I don't push it away—I ask what it's trying to teach me.

Some days, I still fall into old patterns. But I get back up faster. I speak kinder to myself. I remember that I'm not broken—I'm becoming. The shadow is not something to defeat. It's something to understand.

Daily Practices for Growth

My healing is spiritual, emotional, and practical. I pray. I meditate. I speak affirmations that remind me of who I am. I set boundaries with others and with myself. I choose actions that align with the man I'm becoming—not the boy who was just trying to survive.

Healing is work. Not a one-time fix but a daily choice. Every moment I choose truth over performance, connection over comfort, I become more of myself.

The Esoteric Journey of Shadow Work

Shadow work is more than a psychological process. It's a spiritual calling. It's remembering that darkness and light are not enemies—they're partners. The divine within me had to descend before it could rise. I had to break open before I could awaken.

My pain wasn't just mine. It was inherited. Encoded in my blood, my bones, my melanin. But that also means my healing is ancestral. When I heal, my lineage breathes easier. I walk with my ancestors behind me and my descendants ahead of me. This is sacred work.

You are not your past. You are not your pain. You are the one who survived. And now, you are the one who will rise.

Reflection Questions

1. When did you first realize you were living out your family's patterns?

2. What truth about yourself have you been most afraid to share, and why?

3. How has silence shaped your ability to love and be loved?

4. In what ways do you use distractions to avoid confronting your shadow?

5. What inherited beliefs about manhood, worth, or love are you ready to release?

6. How can you show up more fully for yourself today?

7. If you could speak to your younger self in a moment of shame, what would you say?

Chapter 4
The Abyss And The Ascent

Affirmation: ·Every day, I am becoming the man I needed as a child.

1. When did you first realize you were living out your family's patterns?

_____
_____
_____
_____
_____
_____
_____
_____
_____

2. What truth about yourself have you been most afraid to share, and why?

_____
_____
_____
_____
_____
_____
_____
_____
_____

Affirmation: Every day, I am becoming the man I needed as a child.

3. How has silence shaped your ability to love and be loved?

_____
_____
_____
_____
_____
_____
_____
_____
_____
_____

4. In what ways do you use distractions to avoid confronting your shadow?

_____
_____
_____
_____
_____
_____
_____
_____
_____
_____

Affirmation: ·Every day, I am becoming the man I needed as a child.

5. What inherited beliefs about manhood, worth, or love are you ready to release?

....
....
....
....
....
....
....
....
....
....

6. How can you show up more fully for yourself today?

....
....
....
....
....
....
....
....
....
....

Affirmation: ·Every day, I am becoming the man I needed as a child.

7. If you could speak to your younger self in a moment of shame, what would you say?

_____
_____
_____
_____
_____
_____
_____
_____
_____
_____
_____

Chapter 5: Ancestral Wisdom and Karma

The echoes of our ancestors whisper through our blood. Their laughter, their tears, their struggles, and their triumphs move through us like ripples in a vast, unseen current. In the Black community, we carry not only the scars of generational trauma but also the strength, resilience, and wisdom of those who came before us. These patterns—both the wounds and the victories—are the karmic cycles we inherit. They manifest in our choices, our relationships, and our reactions to the world. Some of these cycles serve us, while others hold us captive, looping endlessly like a story being retold until we decide to rewrite it.

Karma is not a form of divine punishment or reward but rather a balance of energy—what we put into the world is inevitably returned to us. It is a law of cause and effect, shaping our lives in both seen and unseen ways. We see its impact when generational wounds pass from parent to child—when a mother who grew up neglected struggles to show affection, or a father burdened by systemic oppression unknowingly teaches his son that survival requires silence. When left unexamined, these cycles shape our reality. Yet, karma is not an unchangeable fate; it is a force that can be shifted with conscious intention.

Breaking the Cycle: My Defining Moment

A pivotal moment of awakening for me was when my third eye opened. I was watching reality TV, high off weed as I often was back then, but something felt different. I drifted into a trance, a mental vortex that I can only compare to the psychedelic experiences people describe on shrooms—though I hadn't tried them at the time. A chant rang in my head, rhythmic and persistent, pulling me into a deeper awareness. When I emerged from the trance, everything started to make sense: the subliminal messages on TV, the hidden symbols, the patterns shaping the world around me.

By that time, I had already gone down the rabbit hole of studying esoteric knowledge, religion, and astrology. But in that moment, it all clicked. I even understood Tarot, realizing how it reflects cycles in people's lives, mirroring the universal truths we all navigate. Some readings are way off, but for those who truly understand, it's a gift—a way to see the karmic threads that tie us together.

Breaking cycles is not a single act but an ongoing process. I sometimes catch myself slipping into inherited patterns—reacting with anger, suppressing vulnerability, or distancing myself emotionally in relationships. But awareness gives me power. Each time I recognize these patterns and choose differently, I reclaim my story.

Grief as a Gateway

There was another moment that cracked me wide open, and it came in the form of loss. After college, I turned to music as my sanctuary. My best friend—really, my little brother in spirit—was sixteen when we met. He had this raw talent for rapping, something that stopped you in your tracks when you heard him spit. I believed in him. Gave him his first ounce to hustle, not out of exploitation but because I saw something in him that the streets didn't deserve to waste. We built a bond—hours, nights, sometimes days locked in the studio, making something from nothing.

I don't think he ever judged me for who I was. Whether he knew about my sexuality or not, he never made me feel anything but seen. As time passed and I started trying to find myself, my energy shifted. I spent less time in the studio. Maybe I was trying to save myself before I could save anyone else. Before he died, I kept having dreams about his death.

Premonitions, I was too afraid to speak. How do you tell someone you love that death is hovering? Especially when we know how the things we say—or rap—can become real. Words manifest. Energy manifests.

He wanted to come with me to Houston when I moved to pursue music, but I had no real plan; it was just a relationship I was trying to follow. We didn't speak much after that. The next time I heard about him, he was gone—shot and killed while I was trying to make a life for myself elsewhere.

The guilt ripped through me. It felt like I had lost a piece of myself. Could I have changed the outcome if he had come with me? I never got to say goodbye. After his death, music felt meaningless. I quit producing. I quit caring. I felt like a broken chord in the melody of my own destiny.

But grief has a strange way of becoming a spiritual guide. It takes you into the underworld, into the void where the ego cannot survive, and only truth remains. His death forced me to confront the part of my shadow that clung to control, to guilt, to what-ifs. Through that pain, I began to understand that loss is a portal. It's the sacred alchemy where sorrow meets transcendence. His spirit didn't leave me; it became part of me. He became my ancestor, my reminder, my mirror.

After I moved from Houston to Atlanta, I made the decision to stop hiding behind the boards and become the artist myself. To carry his memory into the spotlight, to give voice to everything we built together, to everything I had buried. His death broke me open, but through that grief, I found purpose again. It was the death of one version of me and the rebirth of another. That is karma, too. The cycle of death and resurrection. The cosmic law that says endings are never final—they are transitions.

Family Patterns and Their Influence

Two distinct legacies run through my bloodline. My mother's side values success, education, and self-discipline, and many in my family have thrived professionally. Yet, my mother's strong-willed nature has made it difficult to maintain a fully open relationship with her. She accepts my sexuality in words but, in practice, struggles with it, making coexistence difficult whenever she disapproves of those I bring into my life.

On my father's side, the story is different. Drug addiction, fractured relationships, and loss are common themes. Funerals serve as family reunions, the only time many relatives reconnect. I've lost cousins to overdoses and fentanyl poisoning, another painful chapter of an epidemic that has devastated our communities. I carry both histories within me—the drive for success and the inherited pain. It makes me question: Am I a product of my environment, or am I the architect of my own fate?

As my grandmother and I grew closer, she started opening up about her past. She revealed things she had never shared before, including small details about my uncle Tommy's father—though never too much. My uncle Tommy knew of him, but their relationship was strained. My grandmother even mentioned a man she had dated before my grandfather, and though she had been happily married, she still kept up with the news of his passing.

These revelations made me reflect on how my family, like many others, has passed down an instinct to suppress emotions and personal truths. Just as my grandmother hid details about my uncle's father, I tried to hide my sexuality. But suppression in my bloodline goes back even further. My great-grandfather hid his own son from my family for over fifty years. He lived in a small town not far from where my family was raised in North Carolina, yet his existence remained a secret for most of his life. This pattern of silence—of keeping truths locked away—has echoed through generations. My grandmother hid the truth about her son's father, just as I tried to hide my sexuality. Each of us carried a burden we were afraid to reveal, fearing what it might mean for our identities and relationships. But breaking these cycles requires us to bring these hidden truths into the light, to acknowledge them instead of burying them deeper.

Karma and Ancestral Cycles

Karma operates not just on an individual level but across entire bloodlines. Every action or inaction feeds into these cycles, shaping the collective destiny of a lineage. Breaking a generational pattern does not just free the individual; it alters the course for all who come after. It is as if our souls carry the echoes of past lives, and those echoes resonate within us, pushing us to either repeat the past or transmute it into something new.

I have witnessed this firsthand. There was a time when I was reckless in relationships— selfish, unfaithful, and emotionally unavailable. Eventually, I began to attract partners who mirrored the same energy I had once given. My relationship in Houston was a karmic reflection of the chaos I had once inflicted. It was volatile and full of lessons. Through it, I learned that the energy we put out will always find its way back to us.

But karma is not a prison. It is a cycle that, once recognized, can be redirected. Just as the planets move through cycles, so too do we—each decision we make shifting our course like celestial bodies aligning in a new pattern. I started by taking accountability, reaching out to past partners to offer sincere apologies. Not just for closure but to acknowledge the harm I had caused. They forgave me, and in doing so, I began to forgive myself. Integrity became my guiding principle—walking in truth, treating others with respect, and being intentional in my relationships. These became my tools for breaking karmic cycles.

Spirituality and Healing

Healing requires facing these truths and choosing something different. One of the most powerful rituals I practice is self-forgiveness. Whoever your higher power is, pray for forgiveness. Speak the words because our words hold power. Then, stand in front of a mirror and say to yourself, *I forgive you. I forgive myself. I am perfectly me.* Affirm who you are and who you are becoming. Words shape reality, and through them, we claim our power back.

We are not doomed to repeat the past. We are not bound to the mistakes of our ancestors. The power to heal is within us. And as we heal, we heal not just for ourselves but for those who came before us—and those who will come after.

Reflection Questions:

1. What emotions surface when I think about breaking these cycles?

2. If my ancestors could speak to me right now, what would they say?

3. What kind of ancestor do I want to be for future generations?

4. Have I truly forgiven myself, or am I still carrying guilt from my past actions?

5. What generational patterns do I see repeating in my life?

6. What lessons can I learn from my ancestors' struggles and resilience?

7. In what ways can I honor my ancestors in my daily life?

8. Have I made peace with my past, or are there karmic debts I need to clear?

9. What spiritual or healing practices can help me navigate my personal transformation?

Chapter 5
Ancestral Wisdom and Karma

Affirmation: The cycles of my past do not define me. I am creating my own path, rooted in love and intention.

1. What emotions surface when I think about breaking these cycles?

   _____
   _____
   _____
   _____
   _____
   _____
   _____
   _____
   _____

2. If my ancestors could speak to me right now, what would they say?

   _____
   _____
   _____
   _____
   _____
   _____
   _____
   _____
   _____

Affirmation: The cycles of my past do not define me. I am creating my own path, rooted in love and intention.

3. What kind of ancestor do I want to be for future generations?

_____
_____
_____
_____
_____
_____
_____
_____
_____
_____

4. Have I truly forgiven myself, or am I still carrying guilt from my past actions?

_____
_____
_____
_____
_____
_____
_____
_____
_____
_____

Affirmation: The cycles of my past do not define me. I am creating my own path, rooted in love and intention.

5. What generational patterns do I see repeating in my life?

....
....
....
....
....
....
....
....
....
....

6. What lessons can I learn from my ancestors' struggles and resilience?

....
....
....
....
....
....
....
....
....
....

Affirmation: The cycles of my past do not define me. I am creating my own path, rooted in love and intention.

7. In what ways can I honor my ancestors in my daily life?

....
....
....
....
....
....
....
....

8. Have I made peace with my past, or are there karmic debts I need to clear?

....
....
....
....
....
....
....
....

Affirmation: The cycles of my past do not define me. I am creating my own path, rooted in love and intention.

9. What spiritual or healing practices can help me navigate my personal transformation?

_____
_____
_____
_____
_____
_____
_____
_____
_____
_____
_____

Chapter 6: The Universal Mind & Collective Consciousness

There are moments in life where an unseen thread seems to connect us all. A word spoken in the past ripples into the present, emotions stretch across generations, and an ancestral knowing whispers through the winds of time. According to *The Secret Doctrine*, all human beings are fragments of a universal mind, an infinite intelligence that interlinks all existence. This idea resonates deeply with African spiritual traditions, where the concept of interconnectedness manifests in communal rituals, ancestral reverence, and the belief in a shared soul essence that binds all living beings. This is not simply an abstract philosophy but an active force, an undeniable truth that, when embraced, can transform the way we view ourselves, our communities, and the healing of collective wounds.

I once believed myself to be an island, drifting alone through my experiences. I remember a specific moment—sitting in silence after an argument, feeling the weight of isolation settle in my chest—when I realized that my struggles were not mine alone but echoes of those before me. Yet, as I peeled back the layers of my shadow, I recognized that the pain I carried was not solely my own. My silence in moments of emotional suppression, my struggles with relationships, and the echoes of father wounds were not isolated traumas but part of something much larger—an unspoken lineage of suffering passed down through time. In learning about shadow work, I realized that my personal healing could contribute to the healing of my people and that my inward journey was not just about me but about breaking a cycle that extended far beyond my own lifetime.

The Web of Connection

Many spiritual traditions, particularly those rooted in African and Indigenous wisdom, emphasize communal healing. The power of the spoken word, the rhythm of drumbeats in the ceremony, and the wisdom carried in stories shared around the fire are all threads woven into the greater tapestry of existence. In Western society, the illusion of separation is strong—we are conditioned to believe in individual success, personal struggles, and isolated healing. But the truth is, every pain we experience has been felt before, and every joy we encounter reverberates through the consciousness of others.

When I first began my shadow work, I saw only my wounds. The absence of my father, the quieting of my emotions, the way anger simmered beneath my skin like an unextinguished flame. But as I confronted these pieces of myself, I began to see their origins. I saw my father's wounds, the generational struggles of Black men attempting to redefine their masculinity in a world that either criminalized or dismissed them. I saw my mother's endurance, her ability to carry pain while never fully acknowledging it. I saw my ancestors, their voices dampened but never fully silenced. And in that moment, I knew—my healing was not just for me.

The Weight of Collective Pain

How do we begin to take responsibility for the ways we contribute to the suffering of our people? It is easy to point fingers at the structures that oppress us, at the history that weighs on our backs like an unshakable burden. But the universal mind does not simply work through external forces—it moves through us. Every act of suppression, every moment of emotional avoidance, every time we choose fear over love, we reinforce the very chains we wish to break.

I have seen this in myself. In the way, I once avoided deep conversations in relationships, fearing that vulnerability would expose me too much. In the way, I sought external validation, mirroring my father's womanizing tendencies even as I swore I would never be like him. In the way, I conformed to societal expectations, sacrificing my authenticity for acceptance. But awareness is the first step toward change. By recognizing my patterns, I took the first step in severing the cords of inherited pain.

Honoring the Individual and the Whole

To truly embrace the power of the universal mind, we must balance individuality with collective responsibility. Who am I beyond the wounds of my lineage? What do I bring to this world that is uniquely mine? These are the questions that shape the journey toward healing. We cannot lose ourselves in the collective, nor can we isolate ourselves from it. Both extremes lead to suffering—one in the form of erasure, the other in the form of loneliness.

Shadow work teaches us that integration is the key. It is the ability to acknowledge both our light and our darkness, to recognize the inherited struggles and the unique strengths we bring to the world. Practical integration looks like conscious communication, breaking generational cycles of silence, and making choices that uplift rather than perpetuate suffering. The dark and the light, the self and the community, the past and the future—all must coexist in harmony. It is in this understanding that we find our purpose, not just as individuals but as conduits for healing. With each moment of self-awareness and every instance where we choose to respond differently than our ancestors did, we shift the collective consciousness forward.

Reflection Questions

1. How does the concept of a universal consciousness align with the way my community operates?

2. In what ways do I contribute to the collective healing or the pain of my people?

3. How can I honor both my individuality and my role in the larger whole?

4. What wounds do I carry that may not have originated with me? How can I begin to heal them for myself and others?

5. How does my personal transformation ripple into the lives of those around me?

As I continue my own journey, I recognize that healing is not a destination—it is a practice, a commitment, a form of devotion. The universal mind speaks through us all, whispering ancient truths and calling us toward remembrance. To honor this voice, we must engage in practices that reconnect us—meditation, storytelling, communal healing, and acts of service that remind us we are part of something greater. In doing this work, we do not simply heal ourselves; we resurrect the wisdom of those who came before us and carve a path for those yet to come. And in that, we become whole.

Chapter 6
The Universal Mind & Collective Consciousness

Affirmation: I take responsibility for my role in the collective healing process and commit to breaking generational patterns that no longer serve us.

1. How does the concept of a universal consciousness align with the way my community operates?

_____
_____
_____
_____
_____
_____
_____
_____
_____
_____

2. In what ways do I contribute to the collective healing or the pain of my people?

_____
_____
_____
_____
_____
_____
_____
_____
_____
_____

Affirmation: I take responsibility for my role in the collective healing process and commit to breaking generational patterns that no longer serve us.

3. How can I honor both my individuality and my role in the larger whole?

```
...................................................................................................................................
...................................................................................................................................
...................................................................................................................................
...................................................................................................................................
...................................................................................................................................
...................................................................................................................................
...................................................................................................................................
...................................................................................................................................
...................................................................................................................................
```

4. What wounds do I carry that may not have originated with me? How can I begin to heal them for myself and others?

```
...................................................................................................................................
...................................................................................................................................
...................................................................................................................................
...................................................................................................................................
...................................................................................................................................
...................................................................................................................................
...................................................................................................................................
...................................................................................................................................
...................................................................................................................................
```

Affirmation: I take responsibility for my role in the collective healing process and commit to breaking generational patterns that no longer serve us.

5. How does my personal transformation ripple into the lives of those around me?

_____
_____
_____
_____
_____
_____
_____
_____
_____
_____
_____

Chapter 7: The Cycles of Existence—Birth, Death, and Rebirth

There comes a moment when you realize you cannot keep living the same way. For me, it wasn't a single event but a series of echoes—failed relationships, nights spent overthinking, the feeling of staring at my own reflection and not recognizing the person looking back. I had to let go of who I thought I was to become who I was meant to be. And that meant dying, over and over again.

Life moves in cycles. We are born, we die, and somewhere in between, we are constantly reborn. This is not just a physical truth—it is a spiritual and emotional reality, an ongoing transformation that defines our existence. Every time we confront a deep truth about ourselves, every time we shatter an old belief, we are experiencing a kind of death. And from that death, something new emerges.

For years, I tried to outrun the inevitable. I believed that transformation was something external—a shift in career, a change in relationships, a relocation to a new city. I thought if I changed my surroundings, I could escape the patterns that had followed me since childhood. But true rebirth doesn't come from outside circumstances; it happens in the silent, unseen moments when we stand at the crossroads of who we were and who we are becoming.

I remember feeling this cycle vividly in relationships. Each time I was faced with conflict, I found myself responding in the same way—shutting down, avoiding, and seeking comfort in material things rather than confronting what was happening inside me. It took time to realize that these reactions weren't just habits; they were the echoes of my past. I had inherited a way of being that told me emotions should be buried, that self-worth was measured by external validation, that love was something you earned rather than something you simply received.

It wasn't until I sat in the silence of my own thoughts, forcing myself to examine the patterns I kept repeating, that I understood—I had to let parts of myself die. The version of me that avoided confrontation, that sought validation in all the wrong places, that played out the wounds of my past in every new relationship—he had to go. But in his place, a new version of me had the chance to emerge, one that was no longer bound by old cycles, one that could move forward with clarity.

The Death Before the Rebirth

Every transformation has a breaking point. There is always that one moment when you realize you can't continue living the way you have been. Maybe it's a relationship that crumbles in front of you, a painful truth you can no longer ignore, or a moment of solitude so heavy that it forces you inward. It's uncomfortable, terrifying even because it feels like losing a piece of yourself. And in a way, you are.

Letting go of the old me wasn't peaceful. It was a war. I resisted, fought, clawed my way back into old patterns, convincing myself that I didn't need to change. The ego doesn't go down without a fight. And when it finally started to crack, I wasn't left with peace—I was left with nothing. A hollow space where my old self used to be. And in that emptiness, I had to decide what came next.

I have died a thousand times in this life. Each time, I thought I had reached my final form — only to realize I was still trapped in my own cocoon, waiting to become something else. Rebirth isn't about waking up one day as someone new. It's about enduring the slow, painful process of breaking apart, liquefying into something unrecognizable, and trusting that you will emerge whole again.

For me, the hardest deaths weren't external—they were the ones that forced me to confront the shadows inside me. The parts of myself I had long ignored. The patterns I had inherited from a father who had never been fully present, from a society that told me I had to be a certain way to be loved, from the past versions of myself who thought they were protecting me but were really just keeping me stuck.

It wasn't until I allowed those parts to die that I realized I wasn't losing anything. I was gaining freedom.

Rebirth: Becoming Whole Again

Rebirth is not about becoming someone entirely different. It's about reclaiming the parts of yourself that were lost, integrating the pieces that were abandoned, and stepping into your full truth. It's realizing that nothing you have gone through was wasted, that every wound carries wisdom, and that every mistake was a step toward something greater.

For me, this process wasn't a sudden moment of enlightenment—it was slow, messy, and filled with setbacks. But each time I chose to face my shadow rather than run from it, I felt a shift. Each time I acknowledged a buried pain rather than numbing it, I found a little more of myself.

I learned to communicate in ways I never had before. I learned to pause before reacting and to choose peace over proving a point. I learned that avoiding conflict wasn't maintaining my peace—it was avoiding growth. And slowly, the relationships around me started to change because I had changed.

There is a power in choosing to break the cycles that have kept you trapped. There is a power in looking in the mirror and seeing the reflection of not just who you are but who you are becoming.

The Cycle Continues

This journey is not linear. The cycle of birth, death, and rebirth will repeat itself again and again. Each time we outgrow an old version of ourselves, we step into the unknown. And each time we do, we are given the chance to choose—will we remain as we are, or will we allow ourselves to be reborn?

We all fear death, but what if the death of our old self is the only way to truly live? What if everything you've been avoiding, everything you've been suppressing, is waiting for you on the other side of surrender?

You can resist the cycle. You can fight to hold onto what is already slipping through your fingers. Or you can step into the fire and see who you become when you emerge on the other side.

The choice is yours. What are you ready to let die? What are you ready to become?

Reflection Questions:

1. What is the hardest truth I have ever had to admit to myself? Did I face it, or did I run?
2. What am I holding onto that is already dead? What would happen if I let it go?
3. If my old self could talk to me, what would they say? Would they fight to stay alive, or would they accept their end?
4. What part of me is terrified to change? What am I afraid I'll lose? What am I afraid I'll gain?
5. What does rebirth look like to me? Is it peace, or is it chaos?

Chapter 7

The Cycles of Existence—Birth, Death, and Rebirth

Affirmation: Each death of an old self makes room for the birth of a more authentic and empowered version of me.

1. What is the hardest truth I have ever had to admit to myself? Did I face it, or did I run?

....
....
....
....
....
....
....
....
....
....

2. What am I holding onto that is already dead? What would happen if I let it go?

....
....
....
....
....
....
....
....
....
....

Affirmation: Each death of an old self makes room for the birth of a more authentic and empowered version of me.

3. If my old self could talk to me, what would they say? Would they fight to stay alive, or would they accept their end?

_____
_____
_____
_____
_____
_____
_____
_____
_____

4. What part of me is terrified to change? What am I afraid I'll lose? What am I afraid I'll gain?

_____
_____
_____
_____
_____
_____
_____
_____
_____

Affirmation: Each death of an old self makes room for the birth of a more authentic and empowered version of me.

5. What does rebirth look like to me? Is it peace, or is it chaos?

....
....
....
....
....
....
....
....
....
....

Chapter 8: Building Empathy and Compassion

Empathy and compassion are not just ideals—they are survival tools, ancient rites that shape-shift pain into power and transform shame into understanding. They are not passive emotions, but alchemical forces, forged through fire, through loss, through sitting with the parts of yourself that once felt unworthy of love.

To truly do shadow work is to come face to face with your own suffering—and still offer yourself grace. It's not about fixing everything you find in the darkness. It's about sitting beside it, acknowledging it, and saying: *I see you. I forgive you. I love you anyway.*

But I didn't always know how to do that.

The War Within: Where Self-Compassion Begins

I was so used to showing love to everyone else, but I didn't know how to give it to myself. I punished myself long after the lesson had been learned, replaying old wounds like they were on loop. And when I tried to be perfect, to be liked, to be enough—it was never for me. It was for the version of me I thought others would accept.

That's the quiet crisis in so many of us, especially in the Black community—this need to be strong without softness, to give love without ever receiving it. We're taught to keep pushing, to hold everything in. But if you don't feel worthy of grace, how can you offer it to anyone else?

The hardest part was unlearning the belief that I had to earn my worth. That I had to outperform my pain just to be seen. But shadow work revealed the truth: you don't have to be perfect to be loved. You just have to be present.

Self-compassion is the beginning of everything. It is the sacred contract you write with yourself when you stop running. It's not just about forgiving yourself—it's about choosing yourself, every single day.

Community as a Mirror for Our Healing

Healing may begin alone, but it never ends there. Our wounds are rarely just ours—they're reflections of cultural trauma, generational silence, and communal grief. We carry stories

in our bloodlines, in our households, in the places we avoid talking about. Pain echoes through families and communities until someone decides to stop pretending it's not there.

I've felt it in family gatherings—the tension, the unspoken history, the weight of grief too heavy to name. But I've also felt the release when someone breaks the silence. When someone tells the truth and everyone exhales at once.

We don't heal by ourselves. We heal when we allow others to witness our transformation, when we create space for others to be human too. That's what makes shadow work sacred—it ripples. When I heal, I break cycles. And that healing becomes contagious.

We don't just inherit trauma—we inherit resilience. And when we step into our truth, we give others permission to do the same.

The Power of Witnessing

If you've ever seen someone open up—really open up—you know what I mean. You've seen the way the energy in a room shifts. The relief. The quiet revolution. That's what empathy does. It doesn't demand answers. It offers presence.

Empathy doesn't mean tolerating abuse or denying boundaries. It means seeing the pain behind someone's actions without letting it consume your own peace. It means recognizing when someone is acting from their wounds, not their essence—and choosing to meet them with discernment instead of destruction.

This kind of empathy begins within. Because when you can face your own shadow with honesty, you stop judging everyone else's.

Learning to Love the Mirror

Sometimes I ask myself: *What would I say to the younger version of me—the one who waited by the window for a father who never came, the one who thought love had to be earned through sacrifice, the one who believed his queerness made him unlovable?*

I'd tell him: You were always enough. Even in the silence. Even when no one showed up. Even when you broke your own heart trying to belong.

That's what self-compassion sounds like. It's a reparenting. A remembering. A reclaiming of your own humanity.

You are not your past. You are the author of what comes next.

Reflection Questions:

1. What is the harshest thing you've ever told yourself—and would you say that to someone you love?

2. When did you last forgive yourself—and what would it mean to try again today?

3. Where in your life are you still withholding grace from yourself?

4. Who has modeled real empathy for you—and what did they teach you?

5. Are there unspoken wounds in your family or community that need to be witnessed?

6. What does community healing look like for you—and how can you take part in it?

7. Where are you still mistaking isolation for healing?

8. How has your pain become a doorway for deeper connection?

9. What version of yourself are you finally ready to accept?

This is the balance, the work, the journey. And in the end, it is not about perfection or enlightenment but about learning how to love—ourselves, each other, and the vast, aching beauty of being human.

Chapter 8
Building Empathy and Compassion

Affirmation: I trust that by showing up for others with compassion, I am also showing up for myself.

1. What is the harshest thing you've ever told yourself—and would you say that to someone you love?

_____
_____
_____
_____
_____
_____
_____
_____
_____
_____

2. When did you last forgive yourself—and what would it mean to try again today?

_____
_____
_____
_____
_____
_____
_____
_____
_____
_____

Affirmation: I trust that by showing up for others with compassion, I am also showing up for myself.

3. Where in your life are you still withholding grace from yourself?

_____
_____
_____
_____
_____
_____
_____
_____
_____
_____

4. Who has modeled real empathy for you—and what did they teach you?

_____
_____
_____
_____
_____
_____
_____
_____
_____
_____

Affirmation: I trust that by showing up for others with compassion, I am also showing up for myself.

5. Are there unspoken wounds in your family or community that need to be witnessed?

_____
_____
_____
_____
_____
_____
_____
_____
_____
_____

6. What does community healing look like for you—and how can you take part in it?

_____
_____
_____
_____
_____
_____
_____
_____
_____
_____
_____

Affirmation: I trust that by showing up for others with compassion, I am also showing up for myself.

7. Where are you still mistaking isolation for healing?

....
....
....
....
....
....
....
....
....
....

8. How has your pain become a doorway for deeper connection?

....
....
....
....
....
....
....
....
....
....

Affirmation: I trust that by showing up for others with compassion, I am also showing up for myself.

9. What version of yourself are you finally ready to accept?

....
....
....
....
....
....
....
....
....
....

Chapter 9: The Hidden Knowledge Within Us (The Esoteric Self)

There is a vast, uncharted wisdom buried deep within each of us—an ancient knowing that has existed long before we took our first breath. It is not something we must seek outside ourselves; rather, it is something we must **remember**. This wisdom is the language of the soul, the unbroken lineage of truth passed down through our ancestors, encoded in our very DNA. And yet, for most, it remains veiled, buried beneath layers of conditioning, trauma, and societal programming.

The reason this knowledge feels so distant is not because it has been lost but because we have been **taught to forget**. From the moment we are born, we are given scripts—expectations of who we should be, what we should value, and how we should navigate the world. These scripts are shaped by family, culture, religion, and history. And for those of us who descend from **generations of survival**, the burden of these scripts is even heavier.

For Black individuals, in particular, subconscious programming often stems from systemic oppression and a survival-based mindset that has been passed down like an unspoken gospel. **"Stay small, don't make waves, be strong, don't show weakness."** These beliefs were forged in the fires of slavery, segregation, and economic struggle. They were survival mechanisms, but survival is not the same as living. The task of our generation is to go beyond mere endurance—to reclaim the divine knowledge within us that was buried for the sake of adaptation.

The Subconscious as the Gateway

The subconscious mind is the **key** to unlocking this hidden wisdom. It holds the unprocessed pain of our past, the voices of our ancestors, and the truth of who we are beneath the masks we wear for the world. Within this subconscious realm lies our deepest fears, our most limiting beliefs—but also our **greatest power.**

Many people fear confronting their subconscious because they equate it with **darkness**. But darkness is not inherently negative; it is simply **hidden knowledge**. The shadow self is not an enemy—it is a guardian of secrets, a keeper of the parts of ourselves we have been told to abandon.

When we face the shadow, we do not destroy it; we **integrate** it. We learn from it. We allow it to teach us the lessons we were once too afraid to see. And in doing so, we reclaim the pieces of ourselves that were never truly lost—only forgotten.

Breaking the Cycle of Forgetting

The path to remembering is not found in seeking more information but in **unlearning** the lies we have been told. It is a process of shedding—of stripping away the layers of shame, fear, and doubt that have kept us disconnected from our true selves. This process is not easy. It requires radical self-honesty, deep reflection, and the courage to confront the conditioning that has shaped our worldview.

For me, the breaking point came unexpectedly. One night, high off weed, I was watching reality TV when I felt something shift. It was as if my third eye had been forced open—I entered a trance-like state, hearing a chant I didn't recognize. It felt like I was spiraling through a vortex of awareness, and when I came back to myself, **everything made sense**. The subliminal messaging in TV, the patterns in people's lives, the hidden truths behind the stories we are told—suddenly, I could see it all. I had already been diving into esoteric studies, astrology, and ancient texts, but this was different. This was an **initiation**, a moment of profound clarity that changed the way I saw reality forever.

I began to understand that the **universe speaks in cycles, in symbols, in signs.** Tarot, astrology, numerology—all of these systems are merely reflections of the same truth: **we are part of something infinite, something deeply interconnected.** And the key to accessing this truth is not external—it is **within**.

Healing Through Integration

Shadow work is the bridge between **knowing and embodying**. It is not enough to understand these concepts intellectually—we must live them. The process of integration requires us to **embrace our contradictions, our wounds, our mistakes, and our pasts** with compassion rather than judgment.

Self-compassion is more than just self-forgiveness. It is **accountability**, it is taking ownership of our karma, it is rewriting our fate. The obstacle that most struggle with is **feeling undeserving, believing** that because of past failures or shortcomings, they are not worthy of peace, happiness, or success. But grace is given freely. **God's grace is the buffer between who we were and who we are becoming.**

Healing is not about perfection. It is about **alignment**. It is about shedding everything that is not you so that your true self can emerge.

Reflections for Integration

1. What parts of myself have I been conditioned to suppress, and how can I reclaim them?
2. How has generational conditioning shaped my beliefs about worthiness, success, or love?
3. What fears arise when I think about embracing my full power?
4. In what ways do I seek external validation instead of trusting my inner wisdom?
5. What is one subconscious belief I am ready to release?
6. If I stripped away fear and societal expectations, who would I become?
7. How can I integrate self-compassion into my daily life?
8. What message does my shadow self have for me today?
9. If my ancestors could speak to me right now, what wisdom would they share?

The answers are not in the world—they are within you. The hidden knowledge has never been lost. It has simply been waiting for you to **remember.**

Chapter 9
The Hidden Knowledge Within Us (The Esoteric Self)

Affirmation: My subconscious mind holds the keys to my healing and growth, and I trust its ability to guide me toward wholeness.

1. What parts of myself have I been conditioned to suppress, and how can I reclaim them?

....
....
....
....
....
....
....
....
....
....
....

2. How has generational conditioning shaped my beliefs about worthiness, success, or love?

....
....
....
....
....
....
....
....
....
....
....

Affirmation: My subconscious mind holds the keys to my healing and growth, and I trust its ability to guide me toward wholeness.

3. What fears arise when I think about embracing my full power?

_____
_____
_____
_____
_____
_____
_____
_____
_____

4. In what ways do I seek external validation instead of trusting my inner wisdom?

_____
_____
_____
_____
_____
_____
_____
_____
_____

Affirmation: My subconscious mind holds the keys to my healing and growth, and I trust its ability to guide me toward wholeness.

5. What is one subconscious belief I am ready to release?

....
....
....
....
....
....
....
....
....
....

6. If I stripped away fear and societal expectations, who would I become?

....
....
....
....
....
....
....
....
....
....
....

Affirmation: My subconscious mind holds the keys to my healing and growth, and I trust its ability to guide me toward wholeness.

7. How can I integrate self-compassion into my daily life?

_____
_____
_____
_____
_____
_____
_____
_____
_____
_____

8. What message does my shadow self have for me today?

_____
_____
_____
_____
_____
_____
_____
_____
_____
_____

Affirmation: My subconscious mind holds the keys to my healing and growth, and I trust its ability to guide me toward wholeness.

9. If my ancestors could speak to me right now, what wisdom would they share?

Chapter 10: The Divine Current Within

There is a current that pulses through me, one that predates my birth and reaches beyond what words can hold. It is not just melanin. It is a memory. It is intelligence. It is divinity encoded in my skin, a sacred rhythm humming through my bones, my dreams, my intuition. I used to think my Blackness was something I had to defend. Now, I know it is something I was born to honor.

They told us to fear the dark. That Black was absence, lack, deficiency. But I have learned that darkness is not the absence of light; it is the womb of it. The place where everything begins. The spark of creation itself. In the same way that stars are born from cosmic darkness, so too is our power born from the shadows they told us to fear.

My melanin is more than a pigment; it is a conductor of spirit. A transmitter of ancestral knowledge. An antenna attuned to frequencies most have forgotten how to hear. I do not need science to validate this, though even science has begun to catch up. Energy lives in melanin. Heat, light, and vibration all speak to it. That is not coincidence. That is design.

I have come to understand that this isn't just personal. It's collective. It's historical. They stripped us of our names, our languages, our spiritual systems because they feared our frequency. They feared what we remembered in our blood. They knew what would happen if we woke up. If we turned inward and found the divine staring back at us.

And now, I have awakened.

Shadow work has shown me that unacknowledged power becomes poison. That when we deny our own magic, it festers. It lashes out. But when we claim it, when we sit with it, when we learn its language—we heal. Not just ourselves, but our entire bloodline.

I used to dim myself. Speak softer. Shrink so others could feel comfortable. I used to question my reflection, wondering if I was too much or not enough. But the more I reclaimed the truth of my being, the more I understood that my light and my darkness are not at odds—they are partners. And melanin? It holds them both.

This energy is ancient. It is Orisha and cosmic dust. It is the language of hoodoo, the rhythm of Ifá, the pulse of the Nile and the heartbeat of the ancestors. And it lives in me.

Here are the rituals I return to—not out of obligation, but as a remembrance:

- I speak affirmations in the mirror each morning, not just to see myself but to remember myself.

- I let sunlight kiss my skin and call it prayer.

- I sit in silence and invite my ancestors to speak—and they do.

- I write to break the silence, to honor the truths that were buried so I can rise.

- I reclaim the spiritual systems that were demonized, because they are my inheritance.

And so, I walk with a new awareness. I am not small. I am not separate. I am not a mistake. I am divine. My melanin is not a burden; it is a bridge—between this world and the next, between the seen and the unseen.

If the world fears my power, let it. I am no longer here to be palatable. I am here to be whole.

Reflection Questions

1. Where in my life have, I been hiding my power?
2. What does Blackness mean to me on a spiritual level?
3. How has society conditioned me to fear my own light?
4. What ancestral truths am I ready to reclaim?
5. How can I use my daily rituals to stay connected to my divine current?
6. What would it mean to fully embody my cosmic identity—without apology?

You are not just flesh. You are frequency. You are not just alive. You are awakened. And the universe has been waiting for you to remember.

Chapter 10
The Divine Current Within

Affirmation: I no longer shrink to survive—I expand to remember, to heal, and to awaken the power etched in my bones and blessed by my bloodline.

1. Where in my life have, I been hiding my power?

_____
_____
_____
_____
_____
_____
_____
_____
_____

2. What does Blackness mean to me on a spiritual level?

_____
_____
_____
_____
_____
_____
_____
_____
_____

Affirmation: I no longer shrink to survive—I expand to remember, to heal, and to awaken the power etched in my bones and blessed by my bloodline.

3. How has society conditioned me to fear my own light?

_____
_____
_____
_____
_____
_____
_____
_____
_____
_____

4. What ancestral truths am I ready to reclaim?

_____
_____
_____
_____
_____
_____
_____
_____
_____
_____

Affirmation: I no longer shrink to survive—I expand to remember, to heal, and to awaken the power etched in my bones and blessed by my bloodline.

5. How can I use my daily rituals to stay connected to my divine current?

_____
_____
_____
_____
_____
_____
_____
_____
_____

6. What would it mean to fully embody my cosmic identity—without apology?

_____
_____
_____
_____
_____
_____
_____
_____
_____

Chapter 11: Reclaiming the Sacred Feminine & Masculine Balance

The world has done a masterful job of convincing us that power comes from choosing sides. Be strong or be soft. Be a leader or be a follower. Be logical or be emotional. But the greatest deception of all has been the idea that we must pick one and forsake the other— that to embrace both is somehow unnatural, undesirable, or even weak.

But what if the real power has always been in **balance**?

Ancient wisdom knew this well. Across civilizations, the divine was never just one thing. In African spirituality, the Orishas embodied both masculine and feminine aspects of creation. In Eastern philosophy, the yin and yang symbolized a cosmic dance between forces that did not compete but complemented each other. Even in Christianity, the Holy Spirit— often described in soft, feminine imagery—balanced the fatherly might of God.

Yet, over time, this balance was stolen from us. **Colonization, war, capitalism, and oppression tore apart what was once whole.** It taught men that to feel was to be weak and women that to rest was to be useless. It reinforced that men should be hardened soldiers, unshaken and emotionally detached, while women should carry the world on their backs, absorbing pain without breaking.

Nowhere is this imbalance more deeply felt than in Black culture. Through slavery, segregation, and systemic oppression, survival dictated the rules. Black men were stripped of their humanity and reduced to laborers, their value measured by physical strength, and their emotions deemed unnecessary luxuries. Vulnerability became dangerous; softness became a liability.

Black women, in turn, were made into pillars—caretakers of everyone but themselves. The world called them strong, but not in a way that honored them. **Strong meant sacrificial. Strong meant they couldn't break. Strong meant they could never be held.**

And so, the war within us began.

Men who never learned how to be gentle. Women who never learned how to surrender. Generations passing down an unspoken code: **don't be too soft, don't be too needy, and don't be too much of anything that makes you feel human.**

But now, here you are, reading these words. And I need you to know something: **It doesn't have to be this way anymore.**

The Cost of the War Within

Maybe you've felt it. The emptiness of a love that doesn't feel like love at all—because one or both of you are trapped in roles you didn't even choose. The exhaustion of carrying everything, of being so damn strong that you can't even recognize when you need help. The frustration of feeling disconnected from yourself, unable to put your finger on why something is always missing.

This isn't a coincidence. It's the result of generations of imbalance.

Men were taught that masculinity means control, that they must **lead, protect, and provide—but never feel.** To be soft was to be ridiculed. To cry was to be weak. To rest was to be lazy.

Women were taught that femininity means sacrifice, that they must **nurture, give, and endure—but never receive.** To ask for help was to be selfish. To be independent was to be lonely. To rest was to be irresponsible.

And so, we all learned to **perform** instead of simply *be*.

The man who can't say, "I love you" but shows up with money or gifts because that's how he was taught to express care. The woman who takes care of everyone but feels unseen, resentful, longing for a softness she never allows herself. The relationships where nobody truly sees each other—just the masks they were trained to wear.

This is the cost of the war within.

But we were never meant to live in battle.

The Return to Wholeness

Healing begins the moment we realize that power does not come from choosing between strength and softness. **True power is having access to both.**

A man who can **stand firm yet still express love.** A woman who can **give without depleting herself.** A person who knows how to **both lead and follow, both hold and be held.**

Balance is not about erasing differences—it is about honoring them. **Masculinity is not oppression, and femininity is not weakness.** Both energies are divine. Both are necessary. And both exist within all of us.

Reclaiming this balance is not a passive act—it is a **rebellion**. It is looking at the ways you've been conditioned and **choosing something different**. It is learning to listen to yourself, to ask:

- Where have I been too hard when I needed to be soft?

- Where have I ignored my strength because I feared being seen as too much?

- Where have I denied myself the right to **feel, to love, to be whole**?

This is not easy work. It means unlearning, reparenting, **letting yourself be seen in a way you never have before.** It means being patient with yourself as you find the courage to step out of the roles you were handed and into the fullness of who you are meant to be.

Because the truth is: **you were never meant to be one thing.**

You were meant to be whole.

Reflect & Reclaim: Questions for Deepening the Work

Personal Awareness

1. Do I embrace both my masculine (action, discipline, protection) and feminine (intuition, emotion, nurturing) energies?
2. Have I been conditioned to suppress certain aspects of myself? If so, where did that conditioning come from?
3. Where do I feel out of balance? Am I too rigid? Too accommodating?

Healing the Divide

4. How can I create more balance in myself and my relationships?
5. Have I ever felt ashamed of resting, showing emotion, or asking for help?
6. What is one small way I can honor both my strength and my softness today?

Cultural & Generational Patterns

7. What messages did I receive about masculinity and femininity growing up?
8. How have these messages shaped the way I move through the world?
9. What generational cycles am I actively working to break?

Action & Growth

10. How can I integrate both my masculine and feminine energies into daily life?

11. What boundaries do I need to set to protect my emotional well-being?

12. What healing practices (meditation, journaling, therapy, movement) can help me reconnect with my full self?

Final Thought: Who Are You Without the Armor?

This world taught you that you had to **earn** love. That you had to be **worthy of rest.** That you had to be **either strong or soft, but never both.**

But I need you to understand something: **You are already whole.**

You were never meant to live in extremes. You were never meant to sacrifice one part of yourself just to be accepted. **You are allowed to lead and still be held. You are allowed to be strong and still need softness. You are allowed to be everything you were meant to be.**

So ask yourself:

Who will you become when you are no longer at war with yourself?

Chapter 11

Reclaiming the Sacred Feminine & Masculine Balance

Affirmation: I am both soft and strong, intuitive and grounded, fluid and firm —I am whole.

1. Do I embrace both my masculine (action, discipline, protection) and feminine (intuition, emotion, nurturing) energies?

_____
_____
_____
_____
_____
_____
_____
_____
_____

2. Have I been conditioned to suppress certain aspects of myself? If so, where did that conditioning come from?

_____
_____
_____
_____
_____
_____
_____
_____
_____

Affirmation: I am both soft and strong, intuitive and grounded, fluid and firm —I am whole.

3. Where do I feel out of balance? Am I too rigid? Too accommodating?

....
....
....
....
....
....
....
....
....

4. How can I create more balance in myself and my relationships?

....
....
....
....
....
....
....
....
....

Affirmation: I am both soft and strong, intuitive and grounded, fluid and firm —I am whole.

5. Have I ever felt ashamed of resting, showing emotion, or asking for help?

....
....
....
....
....
....
....
....
....
....

6. What is one small way I can honor both my strength and my softness today?

....
....
....
....
....
....
....
....
....
....

Affirmation: I am both soft and strong, intuitive and grounded, fluid and firm
—I am whole.

7. What messages did I receive about masculinity and femininity growing up?

_____
_____
_____
_____
_____
_____
_____
_____
_____
_____

8. How have these messages shaped the way I move through the world?

_____
_____
_____
_____
_____
_____
_____
_____
_____
_____

Affirmation: I am both soft and strong, intuitive and grounded, fluid and firm —I am whole.

9. What generational cycles am I actively working to break?

....
....
....
....
....
....
....
....
....
....

10. How can I integrate both my masculine and feminine energies into daily life?

....
....
....
....
....
....
....
....
....
....

Affirmation: I am both soft and strong, intuitive and grounded, fluid and firm —I am whole.

11. What boundaries do I need to set to protect my emotional well-being?

_____
_____
_____
_____
_____
_____
_____
_____
_____
_____

12. What healing practices (meditation, journaling, therapy, movement) can help me reconnect with my full self?

_____
_____
_____
_____
_____
_____
_____
_____
_____
_____

Chapter 12: Transforming Pain into Power

The Alchemy of Pain

Pain is a shape-shifter. It molds itself into the stories we tell ourselves, the habits we can't break, and the relationships we sabotage. It lingers in the echoes of childhood wounds, in the silence between apologies that never came, in the weight of unspoken fears.

For years, I thought survival was the goal. That if I could push through—through heartbreak, through loss, through the weight of expectations—I would win. I would prove to the world, to myself, that I was stronger than my past. But survival is not the same as healing. And the strength that is built on repression is brittle.

I carried my pain like armor, not realizing it was also my cage. It was in the way I clung to relationships that mirrored old wounds, hoping this time, the outcome would be different. It was in the way I sought validation—through success, through attraction, through being everything for everyone except myself. It was in my silence, my avoidance, my refusal to admit that beneath the anger, beneath the pride, beneath the carefully curated image of control—I was afraid.

Afraid that if I stopped running, the pain would consume me.

But pain doesn't go away when you ignore it. It waits. It grows. It finds new ways to be heard.

The Breaking Point

There was a night when my shadow confronted me in full force. A relationship unraveling, my voice rising, my fists clenched. The words spilling out weren't just mine; they were generations deep. I saw my father in my reflection, his rage, his fear, his inability to hold love with steady hands. And in that moment, a truth struck me so deeply it left no room for denial:

I was becoming the very thing I swore I'd never be.

That realization shattered me. But in the breaking, there was space. Space to choose differently.

Instead of deflecting, I sat with it. Instead of numbing, I felt it. Instead of blaming, I took responsibility.

And that's when I understood—my shadow wasn't my enemy. It was my teacher.

Shadow Work: Turning Pain into Power

The parts of us we fear the most are often our greatest sources of strength, waiting to be reclaimed.

- My anger wasn't just destruction; it was **passion**, misdirected.

- My insecurities weren't just weaknesses; they were **self-awareness**, an invitation to heal.

- My pain wasn't just suffering; it was **wisdom**, a map leading me back to myself.

This is the work—to meet our shadows, not with judgment, but with curiosity. To name our wounds so they lose their power. To rewrite the stories that have kept us bound.

Healing is not erasure. It is integration.

It is standing in the fullness of who you are, past and present, darkness and light, and saying: **I accept you. I see you. And I will not be ruled by you.**

The Ritual of Reclamation

Healing is not a single moment of awakening. It is a daily practice. A choice we make again and again.

Some days, the past will pull at you like a tide, tempting you to drift back into old patterns. Other days, you will feel the weight lifting, the freedom settling in. Both are part of the process.

Here's what I have learned:

- **Forgiveness is an act of self-liberation.** Holding onto resentment binds you to the past. Let go, not for them, but for you.

- **Your pain holds a message.** Listen to it. It will tell you where you still need healing.

- **Boundaries are not walls; they are bridges.** The more you honor your truth, the more you attract those who respect it.

- **The universe will test you.** People from your past will return. Old triggers will resurface. The question is, will you respond the same way? Or will you choose differently?

This is how you know you are healing—not by the absence of struggle, but by the way you rise from it, changed.

Reflection Questions

1. What pain are you still carrying that is asking to be transformed?
2. How have your shadows tried to protect you, and how can you reclaim them as strengths?
3. If your younger self could see you now, what would they need to hear?
4. What new choices can you make today to rewrite the patterns of your past?
5. What does true healing look and feel like for you?

Healing is not about perfection. It is about transformation.

Your pain is not your prison. It is your passageway. Walk through it. Become who you were always meant to be.

Chapter 12
Transforming Pain into Power

Affirmation: The emotions I once suppressed are now the keys to my liberation.

1. What pain are you still carrying that is asking to be transformed?

....
....
....
....
....
....
....
....
....
....

2. How have your shadows tried to protect you, and how can you reclaim them as strengths?

....
....
....
....
....
....
....
....
....

Affirmation: The emotions I once suppressed are now the keys to my liberation.

3. If your younger self could see you now, what would they need to hear?

_____
_____
_____
_____
_____
_____
_____
_____
_____
_____

4. What new choices can you make today to rewrite the patterns of your past?

_____
_____
_____
_____
_____
_____
_____
_____
_____
_____

Affirmation: The emotions I once suppressed are now the keys to my liberation.

5. What does true healing look and feel like for you?

_____
_____
_____
_____
_____
_____
_____
_____
_____
_____
_____

Chapter 13: The Ongoing Journey

Shadow work is not a destination but a lifelong commitment. It is the act of peeling back layers, unlearning falsehoods, and reclaiming every part of oneself—no matter how painful, uncomfortable, or challenging. The process does not end with a single revelation or breakthrough; it is an ongoing cycle of death and rebirth within the self, a continuous evolution into deeper wisdom and integration.

We have walked through the hidden corridors of the mind, revisited the echoes of childhood wounds, confronted the generational imprints left upon us, and embraced the paradox of our being—the light and the darkness intertwined. Now, as we stand at the threshold of what comes next, the question is no longer about whether the work is worth it. It is about what we will choose to do with what we have uncovered.

A Lifelong Commitment to Self

Blavatsky's teachings suggest that each individual holds the key to their own liberation, but they must do the inner work to unlock it. The journey of self-discovery is a sacred unraveling—one that does not promise comfort but, rather, authenticity. To truly live in alignment with one's highest self, one must be willing to face the discomfort of radical self-awareness. It is through this awareness that transformation occurs.

In many ways, shadow work is akin to a spiritual pilgrimage. It is not about erasing the past but about understanding it—about seeing the patterns of pain, shame, and suppression and making a conscious choice to no longer be ruled by them. It is about integrating every fractured piece, every forgotten truth, and every abandoned dream back into the wholeness of the soul.

This commitment is not easy. It demands that we be present with ourselves even when we want to turn away. It requires that we acknowledge our triggers not as enemies but as guides. It calls us to be compassionate toward the wounded parts of ourselves while holding ourselves accountable for the way we move through the world.

But with every layer of darkness embraced, there is a newfound strength. With every old wound brought to light, there is an opening for healing. With every cycle of self-destruction that is broken, there is the possibility of rebirth.

A Moment of Reckoning

I remember the night when my own shadow work reached its breaking point. I had spent years running—from the past, from myself, from the parts of me that felt too painful to acknowledge. But there was no more running. I sat in my apartment, staring at the same four walls I had decorated to feel like home but had never truly lived in.

That night, the silence was deafening. Every memory I had suppressed, every part of me I had buried beneath distraction and denial, surfaced like a tide I could no longer hold back. My father's absence. The generational wounds that shaped me. The echoes of relationships where I abandoned myself to be loved. It all stood before me, waiting to be witnessed.

I wanted to turn away. But something inside of me whispered, *Stay.*

And so, I stayed. I let the memories flood in. I let the grief and rage move through me without resistance. I let my heart break open, knowing that this was not the end—but the beginning of something real. The beginning of me reclaiming my power, one layer at a time.

That was the night I truly understood what shadow work was. It was not about perfection. It was about presence. It was about choosing, again and again, to face myself with honesty and grace.

The Invitation to Begin Again

The path of shadow work is always open to those who seek it. The only requirement is the willingness to look inward. The work is never truly finished because life itself is a series of lessons, each moment inviting us to step more fully into our truth.

For those who have walked this journey thus far, the invitation now is to continue—to deepen the practice, to refine the awareness, to embody the lessons in a way that transforms not only the self but also the world around us. Healing is not a solitary act; it is a ripple that extends outward, influencing relationships, families, communities, and generations to come.

The transformation we cultivate within ourselves has the power to inspire change in others. Just as we have inherited wounds, we also have the power to break cycles. Every time we choose love over fear, presence over avoidance, and healing over stagnation, we lay a new foundation for the future.

So, as we close this chapter, the journey does not end. It only shifts into its next phase, carrying us forward into the next layer of our evolution.

Final Reflective Questions

1. What is the part of myself that I am still afraid to embrace? Why?

2. What patterns am I repeating that I am finally ready to break?

3. If I could speak to my past self, what would I say to them?

4. How does my healing impact those around me, even in ways I don't realize?

5. If I fully stepped into my power, how would the world around me change?

A Closing Ritual: Answering the Call

Now, take a deep breath. Close your eyes for a moment and ask yourself:

What part of me still needs to be seen?

Sit with the answer, no matter how uncomfortable. Write it down. Speak it aloud. Acknowledge it.

This is how we begin. This is how we continue.

The Journey Continues

Shadow work is the reclamation of the self. It is the remembering of who you were before the world told you who to be. It is the journey home—to the deepest, truest version of you.

And so the path continues, not in a straight line, but in spirals, leading you deeper into yourself, again and again. The only question that remains is:

Will you answer the call?

Chapter 13
The Ongoing Journey

Affirmation: I am allowed to be both a work in progress and a masterpiece.

1. What is the part of myself that I am still afraid to embrace? Why?

_____
_____
_____
_____
_____
_____
_____
_____
_____

2. What patterns am I repeating that I am finally ready to break?

_____
_____
_____
_____
_____
_____
_____
_____
_____

Affirmation: I am allowed to be both a work in progress and a masterpiece.

3. If I could speak to my past self, what would I say to them?

4. How does my healing impact those around me, even in ways I don't realize?

Affirmation: I am allowed to be both a work in progress and a masterpiece.

5. If I fully stepped into my power, how would the world around me change?

....
....
....
....
....
....
....
....
....
....
....

Epilogue: A Whisper Beyond the Page

If you've made it here, I hope you feel more than informed—I hope you feel seen. Beyond every shadow explored, every ancestral echo answered, every reflection faced, there remains one truth:

You are not broken. You are becoming.

This work was never meant to end at the final chapter. Healing spirals, not ends. So, as you step forward, remember this: your power is not in your past or even in the pain—it is in the choice you make next.

Honor your rituals. Speak your truth. Let your melanin glow unapologetically. Let your shadow teach you without shame. You are the living, breathing future your ancestors prayed into being.

Walk as if they are watching—because they are. Walk as if you are the light—because you are.

And when the world tries to dim you again, remember this:

You are the son who swallowed the moon—and still rose with light in your chest.

www.ingramcontent.com/pod-product-compliance
Lightning Source LLC
Chambersburg PA
CBHW061158010526
44119CB00059B/852